Retro Family I

Old Fashioned Recipes from the 1960's - 1990's

By:

LeeAnne Jones

I have fond childhood memories of being in the kitchen with my mother and grandmother as they tried out new recipes and baked favorite dishes. It seems like back then there was more time for cooking and homemade dishes were a big part of life.

A few of the recipes they made were passed down from previous generations, but my mother also had collected her own favorites over the years. These were her signature dishes that she'd make for holidays and special occasions and bring to potluck dinners.

Naturally, I had my favorites among those that she would make specially for me, but there were also many dishes made by my aunts, neighbors and family friends that were equally delicious. Every time someone would bring an interesting new dish to a party, my mother would get the recipe and this resulted in a huge collection of recipe cards with delicious delights ready to be made for any occasion or even just if you felt like it.

Today, these recipe cards are all but obsolete with the advent of computers, smart phones and the recipe applications for both, but I still have my moms old recipe cards along with plenty of others that I've collected from various sources throughout the years. For some reason these old recipe cards with their smudged writing and food smeared fingerprints make cooking these dishes that much more fun for me.

In this book, I present to you a varied collection of these old-fashioned recipes that I have transcribed straight from the recipe cards themselves. The recipes date from about the 1960s to 1990s and I hope you find some of your childhood favorites in here as well as some new dishes to try. I brought them up-to-date where needed, supplied clearer instructions and added in some nutritional information.

Even though these are "old fashioned" recipes, I have chosen ones with "modern" ingredients that are easy to make. I hope you find that they are just as delicious today as they were 30 or 40 years ago.

Enjoy!

LeeAnne Jones

This book is dedicated to my mother and my grandmother and to all the great memories, and recipes, they left me with.

Table Of Contents

Breads & Muffins

Potato Pecan Loaf

Serves 8

In 1969, bell bottom jeans and tie-dyed shirts were all the rage, the first man landed on the moon, Woodstock became one of the most significant music events in history, the microprocessor was invented and my mother and grandmother listened to it all on the AM radio in the kitchen while making some of their best family recipes like this potato pecan loaf.

Ingredients:

2 white potatoes (leave skin on)
1 cup onion
1 cup pecans
1 cup dry bread crumbs
2 eggs, beaten
1 1/2 teaspoons salt
A dash of pepper

Preparation:

Preheat oven to 350F.

Process the potatoes, onion, pecans and bread crumbs in the food processor (her recipe says the "food chopper" - I'm not sure what she had for a food processor back then!)

Add the eggs, salt and pepper to the potato mixture. Mix well.

Pour into a greased 9" x 5" x 3" inch loaf pan.

Bake for 50 minutes or until firm.

Nutritional Information:

Per Serving: Calories: 220, Fat: 22g, Carbohydrate: 13g, Protein: 6g

Norwegian Walnut Bread

Serves 8

In 1973 the *Alaskan Pipeline Bill* was passed, U.S. Involvement in the Vietnam war ended, The World Trade Center became the tallest building in the world, Billy Jean King Defeated Bobby Riggs on the tennis court and the *Endangered Species Act* was signed into law. All of which made great conversation over slices of this multi-flour walnut bread.

Ingredients:

1/2 cup all purpose flour
1/2 cup oat flour (you can grind up steel cut oats in the food processor)
1/2 cup whole wheat flour
1/2 cup rye flour
1/2 teaspoon salt
1 teaspoon baking soda
1/2 cup walnuts, chopped
3/4 cup dates, diced
1 cup buttermilk
1 egg, beaten
2 tablespoons oil

Preparation:

Preheat oven to 375F.

The "old fashioned" version of this bread was actually made in cans - back in the day. There's also a special pan that you can use but I'm not sure if the baking time or recipe needs to be modified for that. This recipe is the one that uses the cans.

Grease and flour three 16 ounce cans.

In a medium bowl, mix the dry ingredients. Add walnuts and dates.

In another bowl, combine the egg, buttermilk and oil.

Stir wet ingredients into dry and mix well.

Fill the cans 1/2 to 2/3 full.

Bake for 50 minutes or until a toothpick comes out dry.

You can get the bread out of the can by loosening the edges with a knife or opening the bottom and pushing out if necessary.

Nutritional Information:

Per Serving: Calories: 182, Fat: 27g, Carbohydrate: 6g, Protein: 5g

Scotch Scones

Serves 6

Scones have been around since the 1500's (or even earlier) and the recipe is still similar. These scotch scones are from my grandmothers recipes though I'm pretty sure it's not quite as old as the 1500's!

Ingredients:

2/3 cup sugar
3 cups flour
1 teaspoon baking soda
1 teaspoon baking powder
1 teaspoon salt
3/4 cup shortening (Nana used Crisco)
1 cup raisins
1 egg
Buttermilk (about 1/2 cup - see preparation)

Preparation:

Preheat oven to 450F.

In a large bowl, sift together the sugar, flour, baking soda, baking powder, and salt.

Cut the shortening into the flour mixture.

Add the raisins to the flour mixture.

Put egg in a 1 cup measure and fill the rest with buttermilk. beat them together. Add the egg and buttermilk to the rest of the scone batter and mix well.

Turn the scone batter out on a floured surface. Pat or roll to about 1" thick and cut into desired shapes.

Put the scones on a cookie sheet and brush each with butter. Sprinkle with sugar if desired.

Bake for about 10 minutes - until they start to brown.

Nutritional Information:

Per Serving: Calories: 644, Fat: 96g, Carbohydrate: 25g, Protein: 8g

Whole Wheat Quick Bread

Serves 8

In the 1960's, my grandmother was ahead of her time with this healthy version of quick bread that uses whole wheat flour. Quick breads are a family favorite because they are so easy to make and so satisfying to eat.

Ingredients:

1 egg, beaten
2 cups buttermilk
3 tablespoons dark molasses (substitute honey if you want)
1 1/2 tablespoon melted butter
2 cups whole wheat flour
1 teaspoon baking powder
1 teaspoon baking soda
1 teaspoon salt
1/2 cup chopped walnuts
1/2 cup raisins

Preparation:

Preheat oven to 400F.

In a large bowl, combine the egg, buttermilk, molasses and butter.

In a medium bowl, combine the flour, baking powder, baking soda and salt.

Stir the dry ingredients into the wet.

Fold in the nuts and raisins.

Grease two 3 1/2" X 6" X 3" loaf pans and divide the batter evenly between them.

Bake for 50 minutes until bread sounds hollow when thumped.

Nutritional Information:

Per Serving: Calories: 259, Fat: 42g, Carbohydrate: 8g, Protein: 8g

Side Dishes & Salads

Parmesan Green Beans

Serves 8

The 1970's ushered in many changes - progressive rock, the digital revolution, the home computer and, at least for me, cold green beans. This casserole tastes good cold, but you could heat it if you wanted, the important thing is to let it sit overnight so the beans can soak in the flavor. This recipe uses frozen green beans, but you could substitute fresh, just make sure you use the same amount of beans.

Ingredients:

2 - 10 ounce packages frozen french style green beans
1/4 cup salad oil or vegetable oil
1/2 cup tarragon vinegar
1/3 cup grated parmesan cheese
1/2 teaspoon sugar
1/2 teaspoon salt

Preparation:

Cook the green beans and drain. Put the beans in a large bowl.

Mix the rest of the ingredients together and pour over the beans. Stir to coat the beans with the mixture.

Cover and chill overnight, stirring a few times.

Nutritional Information:

Per Serving: Calories: 105, Fat: 8g, Carbohydrate: 4g, Protein: 2g

Freeze And Eat Later Cole Slaw

Serves 8

I always wondered how Auntie G. always had cole slaw at the ready and now I know she just took some out of the freezer! The recipe is made specifically to be made ahead of time then frozen and thawed later on when you want to eat it.

Ingredients:

1 medium cabbage
1 teaspoon salt
1 carrot, grated
1 green pepper, chopped
1 cup vinegar
1/4 cup water
2 cups sugar
1 teaspoon whole mustard seed
1 teaspoon whole celery seed

Preparation:

Shred the cabbage. Mix in the salt and let stand for 1 hour. Add in carrots and green pepper.

In a saucepan, combine vinegar, water, sugar, mustard seed and celery seed. Boil for 1 minute then let cool until it is lukewarm.

Pour lukewarm vinegar mixture over the slaw and let cool.

Pack in freezer safe containers and put in freezer. The cole slaw will thaw very quickly when it is removed from the freezer.

Nutritional Information:

Per Serving: Calories: 245, Fat: 0g, Carbohydrate: 37g, Protein: 3g

Broccoli Bake

Serves 6

Canned soup was invented in the mid 1800's but in the 1950's and 60's it was really put to use in the kitchen by busy Mom's who incorporated it into many tasty casseroles. Sure, it's high in sodium and probably not the healthiest ingredient, but these are retro recipes and "back in the day" people didn't think a lot about these types of health risks so many of these types of recipes included canned soup because it was an easy way to make a tasty dish.

Ingredients:

1 bunch of broccoli, chopped
1 can cream of mushroom soup
1/4 cup milk
1/2 cup cheddar cheese, shredded

Preparation:

Preheat oven to 400F.

Put broccoli into an un-greased 2 qt. casserole.

Mix the soup and milk together and pour soup mixture over the broccoli.

Sprinkle cheddar cheese on top.

Bake for 30 minutes.

Nutritional Information:

Per Serving: Calories: 133, Fat: 7g, Carbohydrate: 12g, Protein: 7g

Corn Bake

Serves 6

If you like corn, then you'll love this moist version of corn bread. It uses one of my mothers favorite time savers - a boxed mix! I know some people reading this book might not like the use of boxed mixes but using shortcuts like this was something my mother did a lot and I have included the recipe for nostalgic purposes as well as for those that also like to take a shortcut every so often!

Ingredients:

1 cup creamed corn
1 cup niblets corn
1 box corn mix (Jiffy muffin mix does just fine)
1 cup sour cream
6 tablespoons butter, melted

Preparation:

Preheat oven to 400F.

Mix all ingredients in a large bowl.

Pour into a greased 8" x 8" pan.

Bake for 40 minutes.

Nutritional Information:

Per Serving: Calories: 392, Fat: 38g, Carbohydrate: 23g, Protein: 5g

Spinach and Grapefruit Salad

Serves 6

In 1985, Microsoft released the first version of Widows, Americans saw their first compact discs, scientists discovered a hole in the earths ozone layer and this salad made it's debut at our kitchen table. If you need a fancy salad that's sure to impress your guests, then you'll love this recipe.

Ingredients:

2 grapefruit, peeled and sectioned
10 oz spinach, washed and chopped
1/4 pound mushrooms, sliced
3 tablespoons grapefruit juice
3 tablespoons white vinegar
1 tablespoon soy sauce
1 teaspoon sugar
1/4 teaspoon salt
1/2 teaspoon dry mustard
1/4 cup salad oil

Preparation:

In a large salad bowl, combine the spinach, grapefruit and mushrooms.

Whisk together the grapefruit juice, vinegar, soy sauce, sugar, salt, mustard and oil.

Pour the dressing over the salad and toss to mix.

Nutritional Information:

Per Serving: Calories: 139, Fat: 13g, Carbohydrate: 9g, Protein: 3g

Pea Salad

Serves 6

When I noticed this card was dated 1990, I thought "Oh, that wasn't that long ago", and then I realized that it's been almost 25 years! In that year, the first web page was written, the first car navigation system was sold, Margaret Thatcher resigned, Nelson Mandella was released from prison and the U.S. entered a major recession.

Ingredients:

1/2 cup mayonnaise
1/2 cup Italian dressing
10 oz. frozen peas, thawed
1 cup parsley, chopped
1/4 cup onion, chopped
1 cup spanish peanuts
6 crisp slices of cooked bacon, broken up into small pieces

Preparation:

Mix the mayonnaise and Italian dressing together in a small bowl.

In a large bowl, mix the peas, parsley, onion, peanuts and bacon. Add the dressing mixture and toss to coat.

Nutritional Information:

Per Serving: Calories: 346, Fat: 6g, Carbohydrate: 31g, Protein: 9g

Scalloped Potatoes

Serves 6

In 1972, the Watergate scandal was just breaking, the first scientific hand-held calculator was introduced (it cost over $300) and jumpsuits were a popular fashion item. All good reasons to dig into some serious comfort food like this version of scalloped potatoes. I also make a variation of this with ham in it which can turn it from a side dish into a full meal.

Ingredients:

3 cups onions, thinly sliced (about 4 medium onions)
2 cloves garlic, crushed
2 tablespoons olive oil
4 tablespoons butter
2 pounds tomatoes
2 1/2 pounds potatoes
1 1/2 teaspoon salt
1/4 teaspoon pepper
2 tablespoons fresh parsley, chopped
1/2 teaspoon dried oregano
1/2 teaspoon dried basil
1 cup grated swiss cheese
2 tablespoons grated parmesan cheese

Preparation

Preheat oven to 325F.

Saute the onion and garlic in the olive oil and 2 tablespoons of the butter until tender. Remove from heat.

Peel the tomatoes and cut in half. Squeeze out the seeds, gently. Place the tomatoes upside down on a rack to drain.

Peel the potatoes and cut into thin slices.

Dice the tomatoes and add to the onion mixture along with 1/2 teaspoon of the salt, 1/2 the pepper, parsley, oregano and basil. Mix well.

Butter the bottom and sides of a shallow 3 quart casserole.

Layer 1/3 of the onion and tomato mixture on the bottom of the casserole. Add half of the sliced potatoes, 1/2 teaspoon salt, 1/2 of the rest of the pepper, 1/2 cup swiss cheese and 1 tablespoon parmesan cheese in a layer above that. Repeat these two layers.

Top the casserole with the remaining onion tomato mixture and dot the top with 2 tablespoons of butter.

Bake for 2 hours.

Nutritional Information:

Per Serving: Calories: 380, Fat: 43g, Carbohydrate: 19g, Protein: 12g

Orange Roasted Carrots

Serves 4

In 1977, the New York City blackout plunged the city into darkness for 25 hours which resulted in chaos and looting. I have to think if everyone had some of these orange roasted carrots in the fridge, they might just have stayed home! Also that year, Jimmy Carter was elected president, punk music made it's debut and Elvis Presley died.

Ingredients:

1 pound carrots
4 teaspoons butter
2 tablespoons orange juice
1 tablespoon brown sugar
1/2 teaspoon salt
1/4 cup chopped fresh parsley

Preparation:

Preheat oven to 350F.

Peel carrots and cut in half lengthwise, then into 3" strips. Place in shallow baking dish and dot butter over the top.

Mix together the orange juice, brown sugar and salt. Pour over carrots.

Cover the baking dish with foil and bake for 25 minutes. Remove foil and bake 30 more minutes or until carrots are tender.

Sprinkle parsley over the top to garnish.

Nutritional Information:

Per Serving: Calories: 112, Fat: 14g, Carbohydrate: 6g, Protein: 1g

Miniature Meatballs

Makes about 36 meatballs

When I was growing up, every party or cookout had at least one tray of miniature meatballs. What could be easier to eat (or tastier) then a little meatball skewered on the end of a toothpick - perfect party food!

Ingredients:

2 pounds ground beef
2 pounds ground veal
1/2 cup flour
1 cup cream
4 tablespoons margarine or butter
1/4 cup soy sauce
1/2 teaspoon ground ginger
2 medium green peppers
1 can water chestnuts

Preparation:

In a large bowl, combine ground beef, ground veal, and flour. Mix well until blended, then beat in cream and soy sauce a little at a time until it is a smooth paste.

Shape into small meat balls.

Saute the meatballs in 2 tablespoons butter until cooked through. Be sure to turn them frequently so all sides get browned. Add more butter as needed.

Add soy sauce and ginger plus any remaining butter to the pan and cook on low until heated.

Cut green peppers into small pieces. Open the can of water chestnuts and drain.

Put the soy sauce mixture in a chafing dish, add the meatballs, green peppers and water chestnuts to the chafing dish. Baste the meatballs with the sauce. Supply toothpicks on the side for skewering.

Nutritional Information:

Per Meatball: Calories: 116, Fat: 3g, Carbohydrate: 7g, Protein: 11g

Main Dishes

Macaroni Beef & Tomato Green Chile

Serves 4

In 1973, the price of oil went up 200% which meant less eating out. But I didn't mind as long as my Mom cooked up her Macaroni Beef & Tomato Green Chile and let me eat it on a T.V. tray in the living room in front of the television.

Ingredients:

1 pound ground beef
1 onion, chopped
1 cup elbow macaroni
1 cup water
1 cup cheddar cheese, shredded
1 14.5 oz can diced tomato with mild green chilies
1/2 cup sour cream
1/4 cup sliced green onions

Preparation:

In a skillet, brown the ground beef and onion. Drain and set aside.

Cook elbows and water in a sauce pan. Drain.

Mix ground beef mixture, elbows, cheddar cheese and diced tomatoes with chilies together.

Serve with sliced green onions and sour cream.

Nutritional Information:

Per Serving: Calories: 444, Fat: 21g, Carbohydrate: 29g, Protein: 34g

Italian Zucchini Casserole

Serves 6

My father always had a small garden in the summer and zucchini would grow like crazy. Of course that would result in an overabundance of zucchini when they all got ripe at once. As a result, Mom was always looking for new zucchini recipes and this one was a family favorite.

Ingredients:

5 cups thinly sliced zucchini
1 pound ground beef
1/2 cup chopped onion
1 clove garlic, minced
1 cup cooked rice
1/2 cup tomato sauce
1/2 teaspoon dried oregano
1/2 teaspoon black pepper
1/2 teaspoon salt
1 egg, beaten
1/2 cup cottage cheese
1/2 cup shredded cheddar cheese
1/2 cup parmesan cheese

Preparation:

Preheat oven to 350F.

In a heavy skillet, brown ground beef and onion. Add garlic, rice, tomato sauce, oregano, pepper and salt. Stir until combined and remove from heat.

Layer half of the zucchini in a 10" x 6" x 2" pan. Sprinkle with salt.

Spoon the ground beef mixture over the zucchini layer.

Combine the egg and cottage cheese. Spoon that over the meat mixture.

Spread the remaining zucchini strips over the top in a layer and sprinkle with salt.

Cover the top of the dish with foil and bake for 20 minutes. Remove the foil and sprinkle the cheddar cheese evenly on the edges. Sprinkle the parmesan cheese in the center.

Return to oven and bake for another 10 minutes.

Nutritional Information:

Per Serving: Calories: 282, Fat: 15g, Carbohydrate: 14g, Protein: 25g

Cheaters Lasagna

Serves 8

We used to call this "cheaters lasagna" because it tastes like a lasagna but isn't nearly as much work. It's a great dish to have in your recipe arsenal because you can whip it up at a moments notice without breaking much of a sweat and it always tastes delicious.

Ingredients:

1 pound package of Penne Regatta
1 pound ground beef
1 26 oz jar pasta sauce
1/2 tablespoon dried basil
1 pound package shredded mozzarella cheese
1/4 cup chopped parsley (fresh)

Preparation:

Preheat oven to 350F.

Prepare penne as instructed on package. Drain.

Brown the ground beef in a skillet. Drain on paper towels.

In a large bowl, combine penne, ground beef, pasta sauce, dried basil and 2 cups of the cheese. Mix well.

Add mixture to a greased 13" x 9" baking dish. Cover dish with foil.

Bake for 45 minutes, until casserole starts to bubble.

Remove foil and sprinkle the rest of the cheese and the parsley on top.

Bake for 10 more minutes until cheese gets bubbly and starts to turn golden.

Nutritional Information:

Per Serving: Calories: 430, Fat: 53g, Carbohydrate: 13g, Protein: 27g

Ham Stuffed Zucchini

Serves 8

You can never have too many zucchini recipes on hand, especially during zucchini season! I think my mother must have gone on a zucchini recipe hunt as there are quite a few of them in the recipe box. This one includes ham for an interesting taste.

Ingredients:

8 zucchini
4 cups cooked ham, ground or chopped up very small
2 eggs
1 teaspoon dried basil
1/4 teaspoon pepper
1 teaspoon salt
1/2 cup green pepper, chopped
1/4 cup swiss cheese, grated
1 tablespoon vegetable oil

Preparation:

Preheat oven to 325F.

Cut off one end of each zucchini and hollow it out. You can use an apple corer or whatever you think will work best. Sprinkle the inside with salt.

In a large bowl, combine the ham, eggs, basil, pepper, salt, green pepper and swiss cheese. Mix well.

Use a spoon to stuff the ham mixture into the zucchini.

Brush each zucchini with vegetable oil.

Bake on a greased baking sheet for 45 minutes, until squash is tender.

Nutritional Information:

Per Serving: Calories: 303, Fat: 12g, Carbohydrate: 7g, Protein: 20g

Tuna Popover Casserole

Serves 4

When I was younger, it seems like tuna was a mainstay in our house. I guess it must not have been very expensive back then because my mother had a few different casserole recipes she liked to include it in. Unfortunately, most of these also included peas which I don't care for at all! If you don't like them either, you can omit the peas from this one.

Ingredients:

3/4 cup flour
3/4 cup whole milk
2 eggs, beaten
1 1/2 cup shredded cheddar cheese
1 12 oz. can tuna (packed in water)
3/4 cup frozen peas
1/3 cup onion, chopped
1/4 cup celery, chopped
1/3 cup green pepper, chopped
3 tablespoons mayonnaise
3 tablespoons sour cream
1/2 teaspoon salt

Preparation:

Preheat oven to 400F.

In a small bowl, beat the flour, milk and eggs until smooth. Pour into a deep casserole dish.

Mix 1 1/4 cup of the cheese with the tuna, peas, onion, celery, green pepper, mayonnaise, sour cream and salt.

Spoon the tuna mixture into the casserole gently, on top of the flour mixture.

Bake for 25 minutes.

Add the remaining cheese on top and bake until cheese melts, another 5 or 10 minutes.

Nutritional Information:

Per Serving: Calories: 421, Fat: 26g, Carbohydrate: 27g, Protein: 22g

Chicken Potato Bake

Serves 4

In 1965, L.B.J. announced the creation of the Medicare program and the "*Voting Rights Act*" which guaranteed African Americans the right to vote was signed into law. Gas was 31 cents a gallon back then and 2 pounds of chicken only cost 58 cents. No wonder this recipe card was so well used.

Ingredients:

2 tablespoons butter
1/4 cup all purpose flour
1/2 teaspoon salt
1/4 teaspoon pepper
2 pounds chicken, cut up (leave skin on)
2 carrots, cut into 1" chunks
4 potatoes, sliced into 1" slices
1 teaspoon salt
1 teaspoon dried tarragon

Preparation:

Preheat oven to 375F.

Put butter in a 13" x 9" x 2" baking dish and place in oven to melt.

Add flour, salt and pepper to a zip lock bag. Add chicken pieces and shake to coat.

Put chicken, skin side down in the baking dish on top of the melted butter.

Bake for 20 minutes.

Remove the baking dish from the oven and take the chicken out.

Put the carrots and potatoes in the dish and mix to coat with the butter. Spread out evenly along bottom of pan.

Put the chicken back in the pan, skin side up, on top of the vegetables. Sprinkle with salt and tarragon. Cover with tin foil.

Bake for 20 more minutes. Baste the chicken in the pan juices. Return to oven and turn oven to 400F for 20 more minutes.

Nutritional Information:

Per Serving: Calories: 612, Fat: 73g, Carbohydrate: 11g, Protein: 52g

Tamale Pie with Cornbread Topping

Serves 6

The year was 1978 - the average cost of a new house was $54,000, the first cellular phone system was put into service (mobile phones were gigantic back then), the first "test tube" baby was born and the video game *Space Invaders* was released. Tamale pie was a favorite Wednesday night meal at our house back then and now, over 30 years later, it still tastes just as good!

Ingredients:

1 large onion
1 clove garlic, minced
1 tablespoon olive oil
28 oz can crushed tomatoes
15 oz can kidney beans
15 oz can pinto beans
1/2 teaspoon oregano
1 teaspoon cumin
10 oz frozen corn, thawed

Cornbread Topping:

1 1/2 cups cornmeal
1 1/2 cups whole wheat pastry flour
2 teaspoons baking powder
2 tablespoons brown sugar
1 1/2 cup milk
1/3 cup vegetable oil

Preparation:

Preheat oven to 350F.

Saute the onion and garlic in the oil until the onions are clear.

Add the remaining ingredients and mix well.

Pour into a 3 quart, greased casserole.

Mix the dry ingredients for the cornbread topping in a medium bowl.

Stir in the milk and oil.

Spread the cornbread topping over the top of the bean mixture.

Bake for 45 minutes or until cornbread is done.

Nutritional Information:

Per Serving: Calories: 531, Fat: 82g, Carbohydrate: 18g, Protein: 15g

Nut Croquettes

Serves 6

These croquettes make an interesting dinner meal. My mother used to serve them with a sauce, but there was no corresponding card for that. I love a good sauce, but I happen to know that these are quite good plain too!

Ingredients:

1 egg
1 cup milk
1 cup ground walnuts
1 cup fine, dry breadcrumbs
1/4 teaspoon sage (dried)
1/4 teaspoon salt
1/4 tablespoon oil

Preparation:

Beat the egg and milk together in a large saucepan. Heat to thicken slightly.

Add the dry ingredients to the milk mixture and mix well. Let cool to handle.

Form the mixture into 6 croquettes.

Rub a heavy skillet with 1/4 tablespoon oil. Brown the croquettes in the skillet on low heat.

Nutritional Information:

Per Serving: Calories: 239, Fat: 18g, Carbohydrate: 16g, Protein: 8g

Meat Loaf

Serves 6

Meat loaf was a mainstay meal in our home when I was growing up. People don't seem to eat it as much anymore, but back in the 70's most families had it once a week. It's a great way to stretch your grocery budget and everyone needed to do that back then. My mother had a couple of recipes for meatloaf, but this was the family favorite.

Ingredients:

1 egg, slightly beaten
1 1/4 cup milk
1 1/2 cup bread crumbs
1/2 cup celery, finely chopped
1/2 cup carrots, grated
1 envelope Italian dressing mix
2 pounds ground beef

Preparation:

Preheat oven to 350F.

Beat the egg and milk in a large bowl. Stir in bread crumbs.

Add celery, carrot and Italian dressing mix. Stir well.

Add the ground beef and mix thoroughly. Mom always did this with her hands.

Press into a 9" x 5" loaf pan.

Bake for about an hour (make sure internal temperature is 160 degrees F).

Nutritional Information:

Per Serving: Calories: 369, Fat: 248g, Carbohydrate: 12g, Protein: 39g

Beef Stew

Serves 8

In 1986, the worlds first triple (heart, lung and liver) transplant was performed, IBM unveiled the first laptop computer, space shuttle Challenger tragically disintegrated just after launch, and 7 million Americas joined hands in "*Hands Across America*". I bet they all would have loved a bowl of my mothers beef stew!

Ingredients:

3 pounds lean beef, cut into bite size chunks
1 pound potatoes, cut into bite size chunks
6 carrots, cut into bite size chunks
1 cup celery, rough chopped
1 pound can tomatoes
1/2 package onion soup mix
1 cup burgundy wine
5 tablespoons tapioca
2 slices bread, cubed
1 teaspoon salt
1/2 teaspoon pepper
1/2 teaspoon thyme
1/2 teaspoon rosemary
1/2 teaspoon marjoram

Preparation:

Preheat oven to 250F.

Combine all the ingredients and cook in a large uncovered casserole for 6 hours. Stir occasionally.

Do not brown the meat first.

Do not cook in the slow cooker.

You can also add in 1/2 a green pepper and/or some cut up mushrooms if you like.

If you want, you can add a package of frozen peas & pearl onions in the last 30 minutes of cooking.

Mom usually cooked this in 2 large casseroles and froze one for later!

Nutritional Information:

Per Serving: Calories: 404, Fat: 31g, Carbohydrate: 12g, Protein: 34g

Desserts

Mint Surprise Cookies

Makes 40 cookies

I love these cookies because they have a minty chocolate surprise in the middle!

Ingredients:

3 cups flour
1 teaspoon baking soda
1 cup sugar
1/2 teaspoon salt
1/2 cup packed brown sugar
1 teaspoon vanilla
1 cup butter, softened
2 eggs
1/2 pound (40 pieces) of chocolate mint wafers (like Andes mints or something similar)

Preparation:

Preheat the oven to 375F.

Combine the first 8 ingredients in a large bowl. Mix at low speed until a dough forms.

Drop by teaspoonfuls 2" apart onto un-greased cookie sheet - use only half the batter.

Press a mint wafer into the top of each of the cookies.

Cover each cookie with another teaspoonful of dough and press the edges down.

Bake 9 to 12 minutes.

Nutritional Information:

Per Cookie: Calories: 131, Fat: 6g, Carbohydrate: 17g, Protein: 1g

Rum Walnut Balls

Makes 4 dozen cookies

I loved rum balls even as a small kid. My mother would never let me eat too many of them though! This recipe was a rare one in the file because it was dated - 12-22-1982. The 80's don't seem that far away, but this recipe card was made 30 years ago!

Ingredients:

1 cup butter
1 teaspoon vanilla
1/3 cup brown sugar, firmly packed
1-2 tablespoons dark rum
2 cups all purpose flour, sifted
1/2 teaspoon salt
2 cups walnuts, finely chopped
1/4 cup powdered sugar

Preparation:

Preheat oven to 375F.

Cream the butter, vanilla, brown sugar and rum until fluffy.

Sift flour and salt together and add to the creamed mixture. Mix well until it turns to a soft dough. Add the walnuts.

Break off walnut sized pieces of dough and form into a ball.

Bake on an un-greased cookie sheet for 12 to 15 minutes.

Remove from cookie sheet with spatula and cool slightly.

Roll in powdered sugar to coat.

Nutritional Information:

Per Cookie: Calories: 78, Fat: 5g, Carbohydrate: 6g, Protein: 1g

Apple Cream Bake

Serves 12

This is one of the older recipes in the bunch and is one of those recipes that incorporates sour cream (one of my favorite ingredients). I think there was a time back in the 70's or so when sour cream was a big thing to add into recipes and this must have been one from back then.

Ingredients:

1 1/2 cups flour
1/2 teaspoon salt
1/2 teaspoon cinnamon
2 teaspoons baking powder
3/4 cup sugar, divided (1/2 cup and 1/4 cup)
1/2 cup milk
1/4 cup butter
1 egg, unbeaten
1 cup apples, peeled and sliced into wedges
1/3 cup chopped walnuts
1/2 cup sour cream
1 egg, beaten

Preparation:

Preheat oven to 375F.

Sift together the flour, salt, cinnamon, baking powder and 1/2 cup sugar in a large bowl.

Add the milk, butter and unbeaten egg to the dry ingredients. Mix until smooth.

Add the apples and stir until coated.

Pour the batter into a 9" x 9" x 2" pan.

Mix the sour cream and the beaten egg together. Spread over the batter.

Mix 1/4 cup sugar and chopped walnuts together and sprinkle over the top.

Bake for 30 minutes.

Nutritional Information:

Per Serving: Calories: 204, Fat: 8g, Carbohydrate: 26g, Protein: 3g

Applesauce Cake

Serves 8

In 1979, Sony introduced the first Sony Walkman - can you believe it cost $200? It's changed a lot since that first design, and today you can get one that does a lot more for about $50. Applesauce cake, on the other hand, hasn't changed a bit and this delicious recipe is sure to be a hit in your home, just like it was in ours.

Ingredients:

1/2 cup margarine
3/4 cup sugar
1 egg
1 cup flour
1 teaspoon salt
1 teaspoon baking soda
1 teaspoon cinnamon
1/4 teaspoon ground cloves
1 cup raisins
1 cup walnuts, chopped
1 cup applesauce

Preparation:

Preheat oven to 350F.

In a large bowl, cream the margarine and sugar together until fluffy. Add the egg and mix well.

In a medium bowl, sift together the flour, salt, baking soda, cinnamon and cloves. Add raisins and nuts.

In a small saucepan, heat the applesauce just until it boils.

Alternate adding applesauce and flour mixture into the sugar mixture a little of each at a time. Mix well.

Spread mixture into a grease 9" x 5" x 3" pan and bake for 1 hour and 15 minutes.

Nutritional Information:

Per Serving: Calories: 333, Fat: 43g, Carbohydrate: 17g, Protein: 3g

Raspberry Apple Pie

Serves 6

In 1980 the Iran-Iraq war was just starting, Ronald Reagan was elected president, John Lennon was shot and I graduated from high school. My mother made this pie, along with so many other dishes, for my graduation party.

Ingredients:

3/4 cup sugar
2 tablespoons tapioca
1/8 teaspoon cinnamon
1/8 teaspoon nutmeg
3 tablespoons butter, melted
3 cups apples, thinly sliced
3 cups raspberries

Preparation:

Preheat oven to 375F.

Use a two pre-made 10" pie crusts or prepare the pastry for a double crust pie.

Line the bottom of a 10" pie plate with one crust.

In a large bowl, stir together the sugar, tapioca, cinnamon, nutmeg and melted butter. Add the apples and raspberries and toss to coat. Let the mixture sit for 15 to 20 minutes.

Turn the berry mixture into the pie crust. Top with the other pie crust - prick with fork.

Bake for 40 to 50 minutes.

Nutritional Information:

Per Serving: Calories: 431, Fat: 66g, Carbohydrate: 17g, Protein: 4g

Rhubarb Crunch

Serves 6

Our neighbors had a huge rhubarb patch and I always loved the time of year when fresh rhubarb would be plentiful for pies, breads and, of course, rhubarb crunch. This recipe is incredibly easy to make and the crunch topping makes a great combination with the tartness of the rhubarb.

Ingredients:

4 cups rhubarb, cut into small pieces
6 tablespoons flour
1/4 cup old fashioned oats
3/4 cup sugar
1/4 cup brown sugar
1/4 cup butter

Preparation:

Preheat oven to 325F.

Arrange the rhubarb in a 9" x 9" baking dish.

Mix together the rest of the ingredients until crumbly.

Sprinkle the sugar mixture over the top of the rhubarb.

Bake for 40 minutes.

Nutritional Information:

Per Serving: Calories: 158, Fat: 21g, Carbohydrate: 8g, Protein: 2g

Walnut Butter Cookies

Makes about 20 cookies

This is a simple recipe, but I like it because it's easy to make and most kithens always have the ingredients on hand so anytime you have a butter cookie craving you can bake up a batch!

Ingredients:

3/4 cup butter
1 cup flour
1/2 cup corn starch
1/2 cup powdered sugar
1/2 cup walnuts, chopped

Preparation:

Preheat oven to 300F.

In a medium bowl, cream the first 4 ingredients together.

Mix in the walnuts.

Drop cookies by teaspoon on greased cookie sheet.

Bake for 20 minutes or until edges start to brown.

Nutritional Information:

Per Cookie: Calories: 114, Fat: 11g, Carbohydrate: 7g, Protein: 1g

Banana Pumpkin Pie

Serves 8

1982 was a year that had it's ups and downs. The first artificial heart was implanted in a human, the weather channel aired on cable for the first time, commercial whaling was banned, Epcot opened at Disney, cyanide laced Tylenol killed 7 people and the US was plunged into a deep recession. No matter what's going on in the world, though, a good piece of banana pumpkin pie can set your mind at rest.

Ingredients:

1 cup canned pumpkin, packed solid
3 medium bananas, mashed
1/2 cup dark brown sugar
1 tablespoon flour
1/2 teaspoon ground ginger
1/4 teaspoon nutmeg
1 teaspoon cinnamon
1/2 teaspoon salt
1/4 teaspoon cloves
3 eggs, slightly beaten
1 cup light cream

Preparation:

Preheat oven to 400F.

In a large mixing bowl, combine the pumpkin, bananas, sugar, flour, ginger, nutmeg, cinnamon, salt and cloves.

Add eggs and milk, mix until smooth.

Pour mixture into a pie shell.

Bake for 40 minutes or until the tip of a knife comes out clean.

Nutritional Information:

Per Serving: Calories: 247, Fat: 36g, Carbohydrate: 11g, Protein: 6g

Nana's Marshmallow Fudge

Makes about 20 pieces

This fudge recipe was a "new" recipe that my grandmother discovered when I was a little girl. It was unique because it used the marshmallows (she substituted the marshmallow cream or fluff sometimes too). Her recipe called for "oleo" but I've changed that to margarine in here because "oleo" is not commonly used anymore. I think you could substitute butter, but I haven't tried that myself.

Ingredients:

2/3 cup evaporated milk
1 1/3 cup sugar
1/4 cup margarine
1/4 teaspoon salt
16 marshmallows (cut up small) ... or 5 - 10 oz marshmallow cream
1 1/2 cups chocolate chips
1 teaspoon vanilla
1 cup nuts, chopped (optional)

Preparation:

Mix the evaporated milk, sugar, margarine, salt and marshmallows in a small saucepan and bring to a boil.

Boil for 5 minutes, stirring constantly.

Remove the saucepan from heat and add the chocolate chips and stir until melted.

Stir in the vanilla and nuts (if desired - I like it better without the nuts!).

Spread in a greased 8" x 8" pan and cool in the fridge until firm.

Nutritional Information:

Per Serving: Calories: 226, Fat: 31g, Carbohydrate: 11g, Protein: 2g

Frosty Strawberry Squares

Serves 12

This recipe was from my aunt, it was a new dessert she brought to a cookout in the summer of 1992. That was the same year that Bill Clinton became president and California was hit with two of the strongest earthquakes ever. Also during that year AT&T released video telephone for the mere sum of $1,499 and the space shuttle Endeavour made its first voyage.

Ingredients:

1 cup flour, sifted
1/2 cup chopped walnuts
1/4 cup brown sugar, packed
1/2 cup soft butter
2 egg whites, beaten
2/3 cup sugar
10 oz frozen strawberries, defrosted and drained
2 tablespoons lemon juice
1 package whipped topping (cool whip or dream whip)

Preparation:

Preheat oven to 350F.

Combine the flour, walnuts, brown sugar and butter and mix until crumbly.

Spread the mixture in a 9" x 13" pan and bake for 15 minutes. Stir and remove 1/2 cup of the mixture for the topping. Spread the rest into the bottom of the pan evenly and press down.

Combine the egg whites, sugar, strawberries and lemon juice in a large bowl. Beat at high speed until stiff. Fold in the whipped topping.

Spoon over the crust in the pan and spread evenly. Sprinkle the reserved 1/2 cup of crumble evenly over the top.

Cover and freeze overnight. Serve from freezer.

This dessert is a great one to make ahead of time because it will keep for a couple of weeks in the freezer.

Nutritional Information:

Per Serving: Calories: 232, Fat: 29g, Carbohydrate: 12g, Protein: 2g

Kentucky Derby Pie

Serves 8

This is one of the most decadent, but easy to make pies there is. I think normally the recipe has Kentucky bourbon in it, but this one seems to be a "virgin" version.

Ingredients:

2 eggs, slightly beaten
1 cup sugar
1/2 cup flour
1 stick butter, melted
1 teaspoon vanilla
1 6 ounce package semi sweet chocolate chips
1 cup pecans, chopped

1 pre-made pie crust, unbaked (or make your own pie crust if you prefer)

Preparation:

Preheat oven to 350F.

Line a 9" pie dish with the the unbaked pie crust.

Mix the first 7 ingredients together and spread into the unbaked pie shell.

Bake for 30 - 35 minutes.

Nutritional Information:

Per Serving: Calories: 657, Fat: 72g, Carbohydrate: 42g, Protein: 7g

Butterscotch Bars

Makes 6 bars

Can you believe the price of a gallon of gas was only 25 cents in 1960? Times really have changed. Transistor radios were all the rage back then and you could get one for around $5, the cartoon "*The Flintstones*" premiered that year and Chubby Checker started the new dance craze called "The Twist".

Ingredients:

1 cup margarine
1 cup brown sugar
1 egg, beaten
2 cups flour
1 teaspoon vanilla extract
6 chocolate bars

Preparation:

Preheat oven to 350F.

Cream together the margarine and brown sugar in a medium sized bowl.   Add the egg, flour and vanilla. Mix well.

Spread out on a cookie sheet that has sides.

Bake for 20 - 25 minutes.

Remove from oven and put chocolate bars on top. As they melt, spread the chocolate with a spatula.

Optionally, you could sprinkle chopped nuts on top.

Nutritional Information:

Per Serving: Calories: 655, Fat: 94g, Carbohydrate: 31g, Protein: 8g

Printed in Great Britain
by Amazon

Printed in Great Britain
by Amazon

63918591R00128